Ladybird  Readers

Farmer Carl

Series Editor: Sorrel Pitts
Story by Catherine Baker
Illustrated by Chris Jevons

Ladybird Readers Starter Level

Title		Phonics	Sight Words
1	Alphabet Book	A—Z	
2	Is it Nat?	s a t p i n	a is it
3	Nat Sits		an in sit
4	Top Dog and Pompom	m d g o c k	and can I into no
5	Top Dog is Sick		got not
6	The Fun Run	e u r h b f l	at get go has off the to up
7	Gus is Hot!		full his of on put
8	Jazz the Vet	j v w x y z qu	be but had he him she tell was
9	Vick the Vet		did well will
10	Dash and Thud	ch sh th ng	if ran then they with yes
11	Big Bad Bash		big long that this
12	The Big Fish	ai ee oa oo	her look see them
13	The Big Ship		let me my too
14	Martin and Lorna	ar or ur ow oi er	all are for
15	Farmer Carl		cut down good help now
16	The Big Dipper	igh ear air ure	as have like said some went you
17	The Silver Ring		come from so stop we what

First, go through the phonemes on page 4, and do the activity on page 5. Then, read the words in the first half of the book, focusing on pronunciation and blending.

The sight words are introduced in the second half of the book, first on their own and then in full sentences.

At the back of the book, there are activities and assessments practicing phonemes and sight words. These icons indicate the key skills required in each activity:

 Spelling and writing   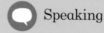 Speaking   Reading

Farmer Carl

Look at the story

First, look at the words and pictures.
Use the words to practice phonics.

Phonics focus

| ar | or | ur | ow | oi | er |

Farmer Carl

sister

soil

hurts

taller

cart

town

corn

down

Aa Bb Cc Dd Ee Ff Gg Hh Ii Jj Kk Ll Mm

Activity

1 **Look. Say the sounds.**
Write the words. 💬✏️

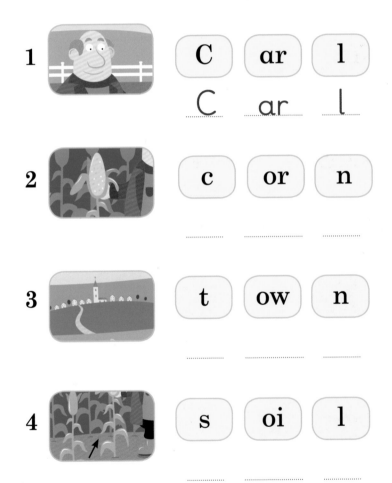

1 C   ar   l
   C   ar   l

2 c   or   n

3 t   ow   n

4 s   oi   l

Farmer Carl

soil

sister

hurts

corn

taller

down

hurts

cart

corn

sister

town

13

corn

sister

Ladybird Readers

Farmer Carl

Read the story

Now, read the story in full sentences.
Practice using the sight words.

Sight words

cut

down

good

help

now

Farmer Carl has to pop the seeds into the soil.

Will his sister go and join him? No!

Carl pops in all the seeds.

The corn gets
taller and taller.
Carl has to cut
it down.

Will his sister go and
join him now? No!

Now, Carl has to sell the corn in town. He loads up his cart.

Carl's sister pops on her coat.
Will she go and join him?

Yes, the shops in town are good.

Did Carl let her go to town?
No! She did not help.
She can not go to town.

Carl sells all his corn!

Then, Carl gets a book.

Activities

2 **Say the words. Match.** 💬 📖

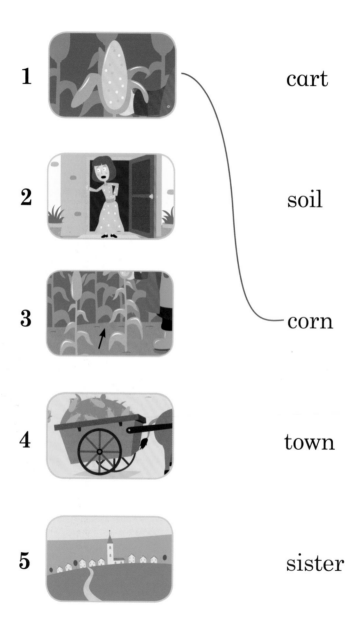

1   cart

2   soil

3   corn

4   town

5   sister

3 Say the sight words.
Write the letters. ◯ 📖 ✏️

> help   good   cut
> down   now

1   h el p

2   g____d

3   d____n

4   c____t

5   n____w

Assessment

4 **Look. Say the words. Circle the word with the same sound.**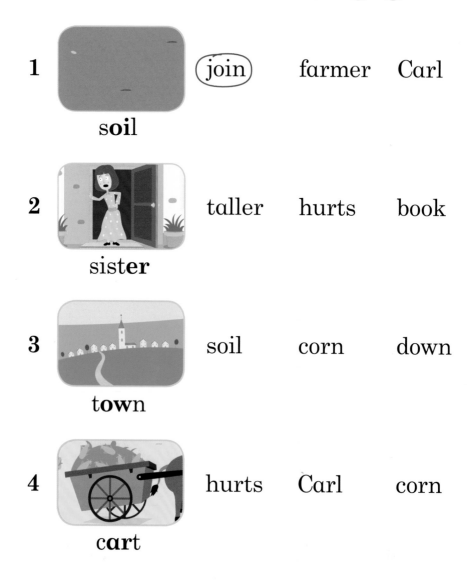

1   soil   (join)   farmer   Carl

2   sister   taller   hurts   book

3   town   soil   corn   down

4   cart   hurts   Carl   corn

5 Look and read. Write the words.

cut	Now	good
down	help	

1  Carl has to __cut__ it down.

2  She did not ....

3  The town shops are ....

4  Carl cuts .... all the corn.

5  ...., Carl has to sell the corn in town.

Starter

Alphabet Book

978–0–241–39367–3 ☐

Is it Nat?

978–0–241–39368–0 ☐

Nat Sits

978–0–241–39369–7 ☐

Top Dog and Pompom

978–0–241–39370–3 ☐

Top Dog is Sick

978–0–241–39371–0 ☐

The Fun Run

978–0–241–39372–7 ☐

Gus is Hot!

978–0–241–39373–4 ☐

Jazz the Vet

978–0–241–39374–1 ☐

Vick the Vet

978–0–241–39375–8 ☐

Dash and Thud

978–0–241–39376–5 ☐

Big Bad Bash

978–0–241–39377–2 ☐

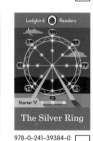

The Big Fish

978–0–241–39379–6 ☐

The Big Ship

978–0–241–39380–2 ☐

Martin and Lorna

978–0–241–39381–9 ☐

Farmer Carl

978–0–241–39382–6 ☐

The Big Dipper

978–0–241–39383–3 ☐

The Silver Ring

978–0–241–39384–0 ☐

LADYBIRD BOOKS

UK | USA | Canada | Ireland | Australia
India | New Zealand | South Africa

Ladybird Books is part of the Penguin Random House group of companies
whose addresses can be found at global.penguinrandomhouse.com.
www.penguin.co.uk   www.puffin.co.uk   www.ladybird.co.uk

Penguin
Random House
UK

First published 2017. This edition published 2019
001

Copyright © Ladybird Books Ltd, 2017

Printed in China

A CIP catalogue record for this book is available from the British Library

ISBN: 978–0–241–39382–6

All correspondence to:
Ladybird Books
Penguin Random House Children's
80 Strand, London WC2R 0RL